world tour
Mexico

SEAN DOLAN

www.raintreepublishers.co.uk
Visit our website to find out more information about Raintree books.

To order:
☎ Phone 44 (0) 1865 888112
▯ Send a fax to 44 (0) 1865 314091
▯ Visit the Raintree Bookshop at **www.raintreepublishers.co.uk** to browse our catalogue and order online.

First published in Great Britain by Raintree Publishers, Halley Court, Jordan Hill, Qxford, OX2 8EJ, part of Harcourt Education.
Raintree is a registered trademark of Harcourt Education Ltd.

Editorial: Sally Knowles
Cover Design: Peter Bailey and Michelle Lisseter
Production: Jonathan Smith

Printed and bound in China and Hong Kong by South China Printing Company

ISBN 1 844 21314 5
07 06 05 04 03
10 9 8 7 6 5 4 3 2 1

British Library Cataloguing in Publication Data
Dolan, Sean
Mexico (World tour)
972
A full catalogue for this book is available from the British Library

Acknowledgements
The publishers would like to thank the following for permission to reproduce photographs:
p. **1b** ©Blaine Harrington; p. 5 ©Jeff Greenberg/Photo Agora; p. 7 ©Robert Frerck/Odyssey/Chicago;
p. **16**, **21a** ©Gisele Damm/Estock Photo;
p. **24** ©Christine DeFranco;
p. **28**, **33** ©Danny Lehman/CORBIS;
p. **37** ©Suzanne Murphy-Larronde;
p. **38a** ©Robert Frerck/Odyssey/ Chicago;
p. **38b** ©Jimmy Dorantes/Latin Focus;
p. **40** ©Alyx Kellington; p. **41** ©Rankin Harvey/Houserstock; p. **42** ©Gisele Damm/ Estock Photo; p. **44a** ©Lake County Museum/CORBIS; p. **44b** ©Bettmann/ CORBIS; p. **44c** ©Steve Northup/TimePix.

Additional Photography by Corbis Royalty Free, Comstock Royalty Free, Getty Images Royalty Free PhotoDisc, and the Steck-Vaughn Collection.

Cover photography: Background: Getty Images/Imagebank/Gabriel M. Covian. Foreground: Getty Images/Taxi/Robert Frerck

Every effort has been made to contact copyright holders of any material reproduced in this book. Any omissions will be rectified in subsequent printing if notice is given to the publishers.

Contents

Mexico's past 6

A look at Mexico's geography 10

Mexico City: snapshot of a big city . . . 16

Four top sights 20

Going to school in Mexico 28

Mexican sports 29

From farming to factories 30

The Mexican government 32

Religions of Mexico 33

Mexican food 34

Cookery book 35

Up close: Día de los Muertos 36

Holidays 40

Learning the language 41

Quick facts 42

People to know 44

More to read 45

Glossary 46

Index 48

Welcome to Mexico

Whether you are planning a trip to Mexico or just interested in learning more about this fascinating country, Mexico has a lot to offer. It has rugged mountains and beautiful seashores. It has ancient volcanoes, tropical rainforests and a rich history.

Some tips to get you started

• Use the table of contents

Do you already know what you are looking for? Perhaps you just want to know what topics this book covers. The contents page tells you what topics you will read about, and where to find them in the book.

• Look at the pictures

This book has lots of great photos. Flip through and look at the pictures you like best. This is a great way to get a quick idea of what this book is all about. Read the captions to learn more about the photos.

• Use the glossary

As you read this book, you may notice that some words appear in **bold** print. Look up bold words in the glossary. The glossary on page 46 will help you learn what they mean.

▲ A MEXICAN MOUNTAIN FROM ABOVE
Look out for this snow-capped volcano from your aeroplane
window when you land at Mexicali Airport. Amazing sights like
this one can be found all over Mexico.

Mexico's past

Before you visit modern Mexico, read about Mexico's past. It begins with the story of great **Native** American empires and conquerors from overseas. It continues with the fight for freedom. Discover how Mexico's past helped shape the Mexico of today.

Ancient history

The first people to live in Mexico probably appeared around 1200 BC. Later, Mexico was home to several powerful Native American **civilizations**. The most important of these were the Mayas, from about AD 250 to 900, and the Aztecs from 1200 to 1521.

Mayan **culture** is known for its astronomy (the study of the stars and other heavenly bodies). The Mayas used this knowledge to develop a calendar in which the year lasted 365 days, the same as ours. The centre of Mayan civilization was the Yucatán **Peninsula** in the east.

The Aztec civilization was further west. The Aztecs ruled over about 500 small states, and a total of more than 5 million people.

The conquistadors and Spanish rule

Native American life changed forever in 1492, when Christopher Columbus sailed from Spain and landed on an island near Mexico. Within a short time, Spanish ships carrying soldiers and settlers sailed regularly to this 'New World', which is how Europeans referred to North and South America.

FROM THE CITY OF THE GODS ▶

This ceremonial funeral mask is from Teotihuacán. Very little is known about the Aztec 'City of the Gods', but it was probably a religious centre of Mexico. The Aztecs ruled a great empire which began about 800 years ago.

In 1519, a Spanish **conquistador** called Hernán Cortés sailed to Mexico. With a small band of fellow conquistadors, he marched to Tenochtitlán, the Aztecs' capital city. Tenochtitlán was the equal in size, wealth and beauty of any city in Europe. Cortés captured and killed Montezuma, the Aztec emperor. He then conquered Tenochtitlán for Spain.

By 1600, the Spanish controlled most of Mexico. Metals that came from Mexican mines, especially gold and silver, helped to make Spain the richest country in Europe.

The Spanish forced many Native American people into slavery. The Native American cultures suffered and the people lost many of their traditions and beliefs.

7

▲ **A BEAUTIFUL STATE HOUSE**
All over Mexico, in government buildings like this one, the elected representatives of the people get down to the business of running their country.

1200 BC
First people
appear in
Mexico

AD 250–900
Mayans are
in power

1519
Hernán Cortés
sails to Mexico

| 15,000 BC | 10,000 BC | 5000 BC | 0 | 500 | 1000 | 1400 | 1500 |

1200–1521
Aztecs are
in power

1492
Christopher
Columbus
leaves Spain

Independence and revolution

In 1821, Mexico gained **independence** from Spain, but 50 years of **turmoil** followed. Different people fought to rule Mexico and failed.

In 1876, Porfirio Díaz took control. He ruled for the next 35 years, helping the country build businesses and make more money. But Díaz was unable to bring about a more equal sharing of Mexico's riches. The people finally began a **revolution** in 1910 to change the government. Their leaders were Pancho Villa, Emiliano Zapata and Venustiano Carranza, who became president.

Mexico today

Mexico is now one of the most **industrialized** nations in Latin America. Its oil and tourism industries generate a lot of wealth. However, most Mexicans are poor. Since the revolution 100 years ago, Mexico has worked to be able to support its people without aid from abroad but it still depends on **trade** with other countries. Mexico prides itself on being a **democracy**, but until the year 2000, a single **political party** had held power for more than 90 years.

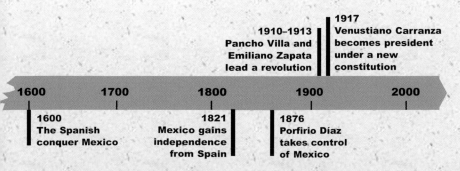

1910–1913
Pancho Villa and
Emiliano Zapata
lead a revolution

1917
Venustiano Carranza
becomes president
under a new
constitution

1600   1700   1800   1900   2000

1600
The Spanish
conquer Mexico

1821
Mexico gains
independence
from Spain

1876
Porfirio Díaz
takes control
of Mexico

9

A look at Mexico's geography

Look at Mexico on the map. Mexico's narrowest point is at the bottom and the country is much longer than it is wide. In some places, only 216 kilometres (135 miles) separate Mexico's Gulf and Pacific coasts. The country is divided into 31 states. Mexico stretches from the dry, sandy deserts of its northern states to the tropical rainforests of its southern states.

Land

There are some important mountains in Mexico, including some volcanoes. Mexico's volcanoes are part of 'The Ring of Fire'. This is a zone stretching from New Zealand to South America and is famous for its earthquakes and **volcanic eruptions**. Mexico City experienced a severe earthquake in 1985. The towering peaks known as Orizaba and Popocatépetl are both active volcanoes and sometimes erupt. Popocatépetl erupted in 2000.

The majority of Mexicans live on what is known as the Central **Plateau**. The plateau is a flat highland region. It stretches from the border with the USA to Mexico's southernmost regions. The plateau is between 1219 and 2743 metres above sea level. Two towering mountain ranges border the plateau on the east and west. The Sierra Madre Oriental is in the east and the Sierra Madre Occidental is in the west.

MEXICO'S SIZE ▶
Mexico is a huge
country. It measures
about 1,972,550 sq km
(761,602 sq miles).
It is bordered by the
USA to the north and
the much smaller Latin
American countries of
Belize and Guatemala
to the south.

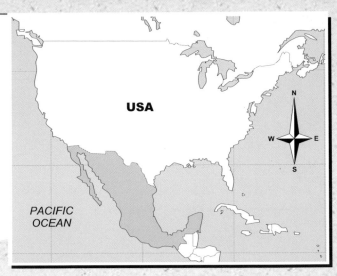

Water

Several very large bodies of water border Mexico. The Pacific Ocean is to the west and to the east lie the Gulf of Mexico and the Caribbean Sea. In the west, the Sea of Cortés separates Baja California from the rest of Mexico. The Sea of Cortés is also called the Gulf of California. It is home to a huge variety of **marine** life, including marlins, seals and killer whales.

If you like the beach, then you will love Mexico. It is famous for its beautiful beaches. Mexico's coastline stretches for 9329 kilometres (5798 miles). Cancún and Acapulco are two very popular beach **resorts**.

The most famous river in Mexico is the Río Bravo del Norte (known as the Río Grande in the USA). It forms a large part of the border with the USA.

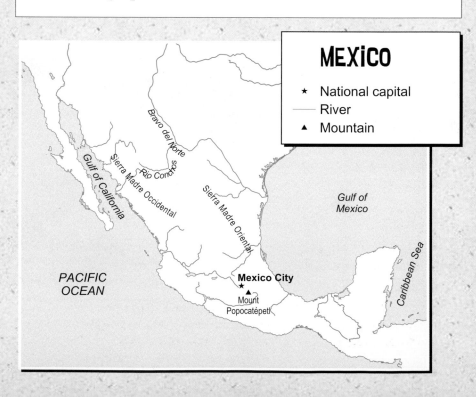

MEXICO

★ National capital
— River
▲ Mountain

▲ CACTI
Mexico's beaches are some of the most spectacular in the world. Make your way carefully around the tall beach cacti, which can be very prickly.

▲ THE BIG CATCH
Because it has so many fish, the Sea of Cortés attracts fishermen from around the world. Too much fishing could endanger the sea life in the Sea of Cortés.

13

Weather

Mexico's **climate** varies dramatically between different parts of the country. The southern half has a tropical climate, which means that there are two seasons: dry and rainy. It is rainy from May to August, and then **hurricanes** are possible until October. In the Yucatán Peninsula, in the south-east, rain falls throughout the year. In the central highlands, home to cities such as Mexico City and Zacatecas, the climate is warm and dry. There is very little rain in this region, even during the rainy season.

The desert regions in the north are the hottest part of the country. In the northern states of Chihuahua and Sonora, temperatures often go as high as 43°C.

The Central Plateau is Mexico's coolest region. It has the country's most **temperate** climate and the weather gets cooler as you go higher up. The Central Plateau experiences great differences in temperature – not from season to season, but from day to night. Daytime temperatures in Mexico City, for example, regularly reach 27°C in the warmest months of May and June. When it gets dark, however, the temperatures can drop below freezing.

Along the coast, daytime highs approach 32°C all year round, making Mexico's beach resorts very popular. It stays very warm at night – the temperature is unlikely to go much below 24°C.

▲ A VOLCANO ERUPTS
A volcanic eruption is an amazing sight – from a distance!
This eruption of Mount Parícutin shows how a cinder-cone
volcano spews lava out of its deep crater.

◀ DESERT CATS
Jaguars roam the desert,
hunting by night, but
they sometimes like to
sleep in the trees. Male
jaguars mark their
territory by scraping the
ground or nearby trees.

Mexico city: snapshot of a big city

▲ **PALACE OF FINE ARTS**
The Palacio de Bellas Artes, on the left in this picture,
is in Mexico City. The palace is a concert hall and arts
centre built of white marble. Some of the world's
greatest performers have entertained audiences here.

Mexico City is Mexico's largest city and its capital. The city and surrounding area is home to 20 million people – almost one-fifth of Mexico's population. Mexico City is the second largest city in the world, and one of the fastest-growing. It is also the highest city in North America, rising 2380 metres above sea level.

Aztec traces

Mexico City's history stretches back to Tenochtitlán, the capital city of the Aztec empire. After Cortés defeated the Aztecs, the Spanish destroyed most of Tenochtitlán. Today's Mexico City spreads out for many kilometres from the original city centre, which is called the Zócalo. It was built on the island where the Aztecs created Tenochtitlán.

The Zócalo is also known as the Plaza Mayor (Central Plaza) and the Plaza de la Constitución (Plaza of the Constitution). While you are there, be sure to see the Metropolitan **Cathedral** that was built on the site of an Aztec temple. You can also see the National Palace which houses the Mexican government. It was built over the ruins of the Aztec emperor's palace.

If you are interested in the Aztecs, you must visit Xochimilco. It is easy to get there from Mexico City by car, train or bus. Xochimilco is 23 kilometres (14 miles) south-east of Mexico City, on Lake Xochimilco.

The name Xochimilco comes from two Native American words that mean 'where the flowers grow'. It is the site of the famous floating gardens (*chinampas* in Spanish). Without enough land for growing crops, the Aztecs came up with a remarkable solution. They built huge rafts out of branches and reeds, then floated the rafts on the water of Lake Xochimilco. The Aztecs covered each raft with mud and soil. This provided them with floating gardens on which they could grow fruits, vegetables and flowers.

Over time, the rafts rooted themselves in the bottom of the lake and became islands. Today, Xochimilco is still an important source of fruits and vegetables for markets in Mexico City, and the many trees and colourful flowers grown there make a most amazing sight.

Modern attractions

The Avenida Insurgentes (Avenue of the Rebels) crosses the length of Mexico City from north to south. Follow the avenue to the Zona Rosa (Pink Zone), Mexico City's tourist and entertainment centre. There you will find restaurants serving the best Mexican food, funky shops, cinemas and all the things you would expect in a modern city.

If you would prefer to visit some of the largest shopping centres in the world, make your way to the north-western and southern parts of the city. There you will find the Plaza Satelite and the Perisur, where you can enjoy hours of shopping and entertainment.

A SIGHT TO SEE ▶
Colourful boats take you out to see the floating gardens of Xochimilco. The Aztecs created the gardens long before the Spanish came to Mexico.

MEXICO CITY'S TOP-TEN CHECKLIST

Here is a list of ten things you should try to do in Mexico City.

☐ Visit the Zócalo, home to Mexico's federal government.

☐ Learn more about the Mayas, Aztecs and other Native Americans at the National Museum of Anthropology.

☐ Visit the zoo at Chapultepec Park.

☐ Visit the campus of the National Autonomous University, the oldest university in the Americas and one of the largest in the world.

☐ Go to a concert at the Palacio de Bellas Artes.

☐ Join almost 100,000 other football fans at a match at the Aztec Stadium.

☐ Explore the floating gardens of Xochimilco.

☐ Take photos of Mexico City's twin 'guardians' to the east — the volcanoes Iztacihuatl and Popocatépetl.

☐ Visit the shrine of the Virgin of Guadalupe, Mexico's most important religious site.

☐ Enjoy a Mexican meal in the Zona Rosa.

Four top sights

Guadalajara

Guadalajara is Mexico's second-largest city, and it is one of the country's most modern cities. Its 1.6 million residents are known as *tapatios*. Guadalajara is nicknamed the 'pearl of the west' and many people think that it is the most Mexican of all Mexico's cities. Guadalajara is the capital of the western state of Jalisco and is easy to get to. Like Mexico City, it is a mountain town, about 1567 metres up in the Sierra Occidental.

Guadalajara was **founded** in 1531 by the Spanish conquistador Nuño de Guzmán. The name comes from an Arabic word that means 'river of stones'. Until the late 15th century, Arabic-speaking North Africans known as Moors, ruled much of Spain. In Guadalajara's central square, you can still see many of the splendid houses built by the Spanish conquerors.

Guadalajara's cathedral, which was finished in 1618, is one of the most beautiful in the Americas. The Degollado theatre is famous throughout Latin America, and the city was home to José Clemente Orozco, one of Mexico's greatest painters. His work can be seen in several of Guadalajara's art museums.

Finally, if you come to Mexico between October and June, the weather alone will make your stay enjoyable. Guadalajara is famous for its dry, mild climate.

▼ MEXICAN MARIACHIS

Mariachi music is popular throughout the world for its harmonies and tunes. These violin players are wearing traditional mariachi clothing, studded with silver.

▼ COWBOY SOUVENIRS

Mexican cowboys called vaqueros made rodeo a popular sport. The corrida, or rodeo ring, is where you will see riders in these boots doing tricks on horseback.

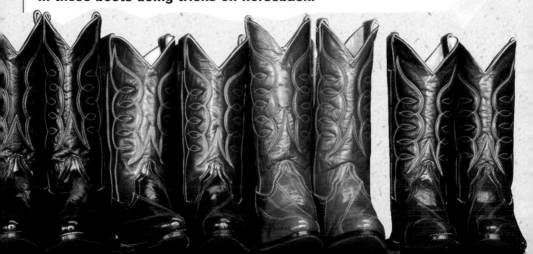

Michoacán: land of the butterflies

Michoacán is known for its lakes, thick forests, beautiful scenery, coast, mountains and delicious food. Even though many of its trees were cut down, it is still one of the most heavily wooded areas of Mexico. These woods are the winter home of Michoacán's most famous visitors – monarch butterflies.

Monarch butterflies are black and orange. They are remarkable for their ability to travel long distances. Each year, as winter approaches, monarch butterflies from the USA and Canada **migrate** south. Millions of the monarchs flutter south at the same time. Some travel thousands of kilometres just to reach the warmer climate in Mexico.

There are twelve separate monarch winter grounds in Michoacán, in the fir trees that grow in the Sierra Madre. The most well known are near the small town of Angangueo. Many visitors come to see the butterflies in Michoacán and say that it is an amazing sight – thousands of fir trees covered in bright orange and black. At some of the sites, there are nearly 10 million butterflies per hectare.

In recent years, the Mexican government made laws to protect the areas where the butterflies live in the winter. **Sanctuaries**, or reserves, are set aside just for the butterflies. When you visit, hire a guide to take you on a tour of these sanctuaries. It is a sight you can see nowhere else on the Earth.

RESTING IN THE FIR TREES ▶
Monarch butterflies (monarch means 'king or queen') set the pine forest on fire with their bright orange and black colours. Go to the mountains of the Sierra Madre to catch a glimpse of them.

▲ TAKING FLIGHT
Did you know that many monarch butterflies are poisonous to animals that eat them? The butterflies feed on milkweed leaves, which create the poison in their systems.

Chihuahua–Pacific railway

Many tourists who like trains travel on the Chihuahua-Pacific railway. It runs between the cities of Chihuahua in the north and Los Mochis in the west.

This railway goes through some of the most scenic places in Mexico, including the rugged mountains of the Sierra Tarahumara, reaching heights of 2400 metres above sea level. To cross the Tarahumara's jagged cliffs and deep **canyons**, the train uses 88 different tunnels and nearly 40 bridges. It took 90 years to complete the railway.

The most breathtaking sight is Copper Canyon, which is larger than the Grand Canyon in the USA, and is home to bears, deer and several species of reptile.

FASCINATING FACT

Chihuahuas are the smallest dogs in the world. They grow only about 13 centimetres tall. These little dogs come from Mexico. They were named after the city of Chihuahua.

▲ **COPPER CANYON**
Go aboard the Chihuahua-Pacific railway for a trip through Sierra Tarahumara. There you will find waterfalls, flower gardens and historic sites.

Yucatán Peninsula

Although the Yucatán Peninsula is part of Mexico, visitors often think it is like a separate country. The Yucatán was home to the Mayan civilisation. Many of the people who live in Yucatán have Mayan ancestors and several of the Mayan languages are still spoken here.

Uxmal and Chichén Itzá are the ruins of two great Mayan cities. Both are close to the present-day city of Mérida.

Most of the Yucatán enjoys a tropical climate. It is a good place to spot tropical plant and animal life. The peninsula is particularly famous for its brightly coloured birds and is a great place to enjoy bird-watching.

◀ A TROPICAL DISPLAY
One of the delights of visiting Mexico is seeing its exotic wildlife. You can see beautiful coloured birds everywhere, high up in the trees.

▲ IN THE HISTORIC YUCATÁN
The Mayan civilization left behind many clues about
its culture. Mayan priests used temples like this one
for religious ceremonies and sacrifices to the gods.

Going to school in Mexico

Mexico's government funds public schools throughout Mexico. Most Mexican children attend school only from the ages of six to fourteen. In many places in the country, there are no schools for children who are older than fourteen. More than 15 per cent of Mexican children do not attend school at all. Between 85 per cent and 90 per cent of Mexican adults can read and write.

▲ GOING TO SCHOOL IN MEXICO
Classes in Mexico are taught in Spanish, the national language.

Mexicans enjoy all kinds of sports. The official national sport is bullfighting and the Plaza Mexico in Mexico City is the largest bullring in the world.

Bullfighting might be Mexico's official national sport, but its most popular sport is football. Mexicans of all ages and backgrounds play football. The country has a fabulous professional league. Its national team often qualifies for the football World Cup.

Baseball is also a popular sport in Mexico. Many Mexican players now play in major league baseball teams in the USA.

Boxing is another very popular sport in Mexico. Mexican fighters, such as Julio Cesar Chavez and Salvador Sanchez, have been world champions.

▲ A BULLFIGHT
Bullfighting in Mexico began during Spanish rule and is still popular today. It is a dangerous sport. The matadors – bullfighters – have to be very brave and graceful to survive.

From farming to factories

Modern Mexico is an industrial country with many factories and large businesses. Mexico's most important product is petroleum (natural gas and oil) because Mexico has the fifth-largest **oil reserves** in the world. The sale of oil accounts for more than 70 per cent of the money earned from **exports**. The kind of money used in Mexico is called the peso.

Many people think of Mexico as a land of farmers who work small pieces of land. This is still true in parts of the country, but only 20 per cent of Mexicans earn a living from farming. Farmed products, like sugar and coffee, remain an important part of the **economy**. In recent years, flowers have become another important Mexican export.

Every year, more and more Mexicans move into factory work. Most factories are found in the north, near the border with the USA. Factories called *maquiladoras* produce pieces and parts for companies in the USA. They make all kinds of things from car parts to clothing.

Tourists are a very important part of the Mexican economy. The tourists who come to see the monarch butterflies in Michoacán, to enjoy the sand and sea at Cancún or to visit Mayan ruins in the Yucatán all provide jobs for people who work as tour guides or in transport, restaurants, shops and hotels.

▲ **THAT IS A LOT OF TRAFFIC**
Mexico's roads are jam-packed with Volkswagen 'beetle' taxis.

TOURING THE YUCATÁN ▶
Mexico's beaches are lined
with luxurious resorts.
Cancún, shown in this
photo, and the ancient
Mayan temple at nearby
Tulúm draw tourists from all
over the world.

The Mexican government

Mexico is a federal **republic**. It consists of 31 states and the Federal District of Mexico City. The Constitution of 1917 is the basis of the laws of Mexico. All Mexicans over eighteen have the right to vote. In fact, they have to vote. People who do not vote in elections may be required to pay a fine.

Mexico has a president and two houses of the legislature. The people directly elect the president. He or she can serve only one six-year term.

The president is the most powerful political figure in Mexico. He or she appoints people to fill all major political offices.

The legislature is made up of two parts that are called houses: the Senate has 128 members and the Chamber of Deputies has more than 500 members.

MEXICO'S NATIONAL FLAG

The Mexican flag is called La Bandera de México. It symbolizes Mexico's rich Aztec heritage. According to legend, the Aztecs were looking for a place to build their empire when they first came to Mexico. They were looking for an eagle perched on a prickly pear tree eating a serpent, and they found it in the place known today as Mexico.

Religions of Mexico

The Constitution of 1917 guarantees a separation of church and state. This means that Mexico has no official religion. However, more than 89 per cent of Mexicans are Roman Catholic, the church the conquistadors brought to Mexico.

For Mexico's Catholics, the most sacred site in the country is the shrine of the Virgin of Guadalupe near Mexico City. The shrine honours what Catholics believe was the appearance of the Virgin Mary to a Mexican peasant named Juan Diego in 1531. The Virgin of Guadalupe is often pictured with dark skin and in poor clothing as if she were a Mexican peasant herself. She is Mexico's patron saint. She also became the symbol of the independence movement in the 19th century.

A small number of Mexicans follow other religions. Some are Jewish, some are Muslim and others are Protestant Christians.

▲ THE SHRINE OF THE VIRGIN OF GUADALUPE
When Juan Diego claimed to see the Virgin Mary in Mexico City, many Catholics flocked to the site. The shrine has now become a sacred and holy place.

Mexican food

The food eaten by most Mexican people is tasty and simple. Many dishes include those foods grown by Mexican farmers, such as maize, rice, beans and chillis. Of these, maize is the most common and the most important. Many Mexicans eat maize every day of their lives, most often in the form of tortillas (very thin rounds of bread, usually eaten with a topping or filling).

Rice is relatively easy to grow in the mountains and in tropical regions. In the north of Mexico, wheat is more commonly grown. Chillies are hot peppers. More than 150 different kinds of chilli grow in Mexico. They are used most often as a spice or seasoning, but some large chillies are stuffed and baked.

▲ DINNER, MEXICAN STYLE
Tortilla chips and salsa, with a little guacamole (avocado dip), and some rice and beans, make a complete Mexican meal.

Mexico's recipe

SALSA CRUDA

INGREDIENTS:

1 small onion or 6 spring onions
4 large, ripe tomatoes
Juice of 1 lime
Salt
Coriander leaves
2 mild chillies

WARNING:

Never cook or bake by yourself. Always ask an adult to help you in the kitchen. Wash your hands after handling chillies, and do not get chillies near your eyes.

DIRECTIONS:

Chop the onions and the chillies. Put them into a bowl. Add the lime juice and a pinch of salt. Chop the tomatoes and coriander leaves into very small pieces. Add them to the bowl. Mix everything together with a spoon. Leave the mixture for five minutes. Taste it and add more salt if you think it needs it. Salsa is served with most meals in Mexico. This recipe is for salsa cruda, which means 'simple sauce'.

Up close: Dia de los Muertos

Mexicans have been celebrating Día de los Muertos (Day of the Dead) for over 3000 years. The Aztecs traditionally held feast days that were dedicated to remembering the dead and two months of their calendar were set aside to remember the dead and honour their ancestors.

The Aztecs respected death, but perhaps did not fear it. All people have death in common. For this reason, the Day of the Dead is a joyful occasion, not a sad one. It is a time for feasting, celebrating and remembering the best things about relatives and friends who have died.

All Saints and All Souls

After the Spanish conquistadors arrived, Catholic priests in Mexico tried to abolish the Day of the Dead. They thought it was unholy. But the tradition proved too strong to remove completely. Instead, it became associated with two Catholic holy days: All Saints Day, on 1 November, and All Souls Day, on 2 November.

As more Mexicans converted to Catholicism, they celebrated the traditional feast on Catholic holy days. Today, the Day of the Dead celebrations have both Catholic and traditional parts.

Many think that the Day of the Dead is similar to a Hallowe'en celebration because people wear scary masks (usually of skeletons) and exchange gifts and sweets and other treats but in fact it is a very different occasion.

▲ SPENDING TIME WITH THE SPIRITS
This altar is built to honour the dead on the Mexican holiday
called Día de los Muertos, the Day of the Dead. Families
visit the graves of their friends and relatives, bringing
flowers, food and their loved ones' favourite things.

▲ DAY OF THE DEAD IN TZINTZUNTZAN
The town of Tzintzuntzan remembers its dead with an all-night vigil. It is a happy occasion for remembering good things about their families.

◀ SPECIAL SWEETS
You'll find treats like this decorated sugar skull at any Day of the Dead celebration.

How it is celebrated

Both 1 and 2 November are set aside to remember dead relatives and friends. The way that the holiday is celebrated varies from place to place in Mexico.

In general, 1 November is set aside for remembering people who died as children, and 2 November celebrates those who died when they were adults. Families usually gather together on both days for a festive meal or to attend Mass – a religious gathering at a Catholic church. They may leave offerings of food and drink at specially made **altars** in their homes. Families may visit the graves of loved ones. There they eat, drink, sing and tell stories about the dead.

Special foods, such as *pan de muerto* (bread of the dead) and sugary skeleton sweets, are made and eaten. People dress up in colourful costumes and masks, usually of skeletons. In some parts of the country, families spend all night in the cemetery and keep watch by candlelight for the return of the departed spirits.

Holidays

One of Mexico's national holidays is Independence Day, on 16 September. This public holiday celebrates the day in 1810 when Mexico began its rebellion against Spanish rule and Mexicans spend the day enjoying parades, food and fireworks.

Mexicans also celebrate Cinco de Mayo (Fifth of May) which commemorates Mexico's defeat of the French army that tried to invade it in 1862. This holiday is also marked with parades, fireworks, a lot of eating and drinking and music.

Mexico has no official religion but people celebrate many religious holidays. The Day of the Dead includes elements of both Catholic holy days and native Mexican traditions. Other important religious holidays are Christmas and Easter. Mexicans also observe Catholic feast days that honour the Virgin Mary. These are celebrated by attending Mass and other religious services, and by eating a meal and spending time with family.

◀ **DANCE OF THE VIEJITOS**
Viejitos means 'old men' in Spanish. This dance is performed on Día de la Candelaria, or Day of the Candles. It is a time of purification and is part of the Mexican Christmas tradition.

Learning the language

English	Spanish	How to say it
What's your name?	Como se llama usted?	KO-mo seh JA-ma OOS-tehd
My name is _____	Me llamo _____	MEH JA-mo _____
Where are you from?	¿De donde es usted?	DE DOHN-de ES OOS-tehd
I'm from _____	Soy de _____	SOY de _____
Thank you	Gracias	GRAH-see-ahs
You're welcome	De nada / A la orden	DEH NAW-da/ AH LAH OR-den
I speak little Spanish	Hablo un poco de español	AHB-lo OON PO-ko DE ESS-pah-nyol

Quick facts

Mexico

Capital
Mexico City

Borders
Belize, Guatemala, USA

Area
1,972,550 sq km
(761,602 sq miles)

Population
103,400,165

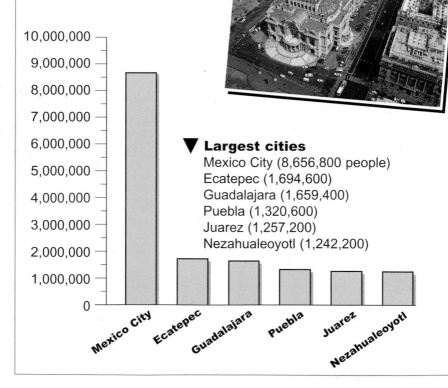

▼ **Largest cities**
Mexico City (8,656,800 people)
Ecatepec (1,694,600)
Guadalajara (1,659,400)
Puebla (1,320,600)
Juarez (1,257,200)
Nezahualeoyotl (1,242,200)

▲ Flag of Mexico

Longest river
Río Bravo del Norte
3060 km (1900 miles)
long

Coastline ▶
9329 km (5798 miles)

Literacy rate
89.6% of Mexicans
can read

Natural resources
Oil and natural gas,
silver, copper, gold, lead,
zinc, timber

▼ Monetary unit
Mexican peso

Major industries
Food and beverages, tobacco,
chemicals, iron and steel, petroleum
mining, textiles, clothing, motor
vehicles, consumer durables,
tourism

Chief crops and livestock
Maize, wheat, soyabeans, rice,
beans, cotton, coffee, fruit,
tomatoes, cattle, poultry

People to know

◀ Emiliano Zapata

Emiliano Zapata (1879–1919) was a *mestizo* (of mixed Spanish and Native American blood) peasant who led protests in his home village when rich landowners seized the peasants' land. During the Mexican Revolution, his forces took land stolen by plantation owners and gave it back to the poor.

Frida Kahlo ▶

Frida Kahlo (1907–1954) was a painter and was best known for her use of bright, vibrant colour in her many self-portraits. Kahlo taught herself to paint while recovering from a bus accident that caused her to undergo 35 operations.

◀ Octavio Paz

Octavio Paz was a poet, essayist and diplomat. He was one of the most important Spanish-language writers. His essay 'The Labyrinth of Solitude' is one of the best explanations of Mexico's history, character and culture. Paz was awarded the Nobel Prize for Literature in 1990.

More to read

Do you want to know more about Mexico? Have a look at the books below.

Nations of the World: Mexico, Jen Green
    (Raintree, 2003)
Explore the history and identity of Mexican communities by looking at the culture, economy and geography of Mexico.

A World of Recipes: Mexico, Julie McCulloch
    (Heinemann Library, 2001)
Learn how Mexicans used ingredients like turkey, sweetcorn, tomatoes, peppers, peanuts and chocolate for hundreds of years before they were known in Europe. Learn what tortillas, nachos and enchilladas are and how to make them.

See through History: The Aztecs, Tim Wood
    (Heinemann Library, 1992)
Discover life in the Aztec Empire. Peel back see-through pages to look inside the Great Temple of Tenochtitlán, an Aztec house, a magnificent palace and a temple of the Aztec Knights.

The Life and World of Montezuma, Stuart Reid
    (Heinemann Library, 2002)
Read the life story of Montezuma. Find out who he was, when and where he lived and what he was famous for.

Glossary

altar raised platform used in religious ceremonies

canyon deep and narrow river valley with steep, rocky sides

cathedral very large church, often built in the shape of a cross

civilization society that has its own language, arts, customs and power structure

climate typical weather in a place

conquistador (kone-KEES-tah-dor) 16th-century Spanish soldier. The conquistadors defeated the Native American civilizations of Mexico, Central America and Peru

culture way of life of a society or civilization

democracy type of government in which the people vote for their officials

economy country's way of running its industry, trade and businesses

export product sent to another country for sale

founded to have started or set up something

hurricane dangerous and violent storm that brings strong winds and heavy rains

independence state of being self-governing

industrialized having many businesses and factories for making things

legislature part of a government that makes the laws

marine having to do with the sea

migrate to move from one place to another

native belonging by birth or origin to a place

oil reserves oil that is stored for future use

peninsula area of land that is surrounded by water on all but one side

plateau high, flat area of land

political party group of people who share the same values and support candidates for election

republic form of government without a monarch, in which the people vote for their leaders

resort place where people go on holiday

revolution complete change in government, usually brought about by the people

sanctuary protected area of land where endangered animals are kept safe

temperate not too hot or too cold

trade buying and selling of goods

turmoil uproar and confusion

volcanic eruption explosion of hot lava, ashes and rocks from deep inside a volcano

Index

Aztec 6, 7, 8, 17, 18, 19, 32, 36

bullfighting 19, 29
butterfly, monarch 22, 23

Cancún 11, 12, 30, 31
Carranza, Venustiano 9
Catholic 33, 36, 39, 40
Chichén Itzá 26
Chihuahua 11, 14, 24, 25
Columbus, Christopher 6, 8
conquistador 7, 20, 36
Copper Canyon 24, 25
Cortés, Hernán 7, 8, 17

Day of the Dead (Día de los
    Muertos) 36, 37, 38, 39, 40
Díaz, Porfirio 9

Floating garden 18, 19

Guadalajara 11, 20, 42

Kahlo, Frida 44

mariachi 21
Mayas, Mayan 6, 8, 19, 26, 27,
    30, 31
Mexico City 10, 11, 12, 14, 16,
    17, 18, 19, 20, 29, 42
Michoácan 22
mine 7, 43
Montezuma 7

National Museum of
    Anthropology 19

oil 30, 43
Orizaba (volcano) 10
Orozco, José Clemente 20

Palace of Fine Arts 16
Paz, Octavio 44
Popocatépetl (volcano) 10, 19

Río Grande 12
rodeo 21

Sea of Cortés 12, 13
Spain, Spanish rule 6, 7, 8, 9,
    17, 20, 29, 36, 40

Tenochtitlán 7

USA 10, 11, 12, 22, 29, 30, 42
Uxmal 26

Villa, Pancho 9
Virgin of Guadalupe 33
volcano 5, 10, 15, 19

Xochimilco 17, 18, 19

Yucatán Peninsula 6, 11, 14,
    26, 27, 30, 31

Zapata, Emiliano 9, 44